Hopkins on Skellig Michael

poems by

Paddy Bushe

DEDALUS

The Dedalus Press
24 The Heath ~ Cypress Downs ~ Dublin 6W
www.dedaluspoetry.com

Cover: "Steps to Summit: The Skelligs", reproduced courtesy of Dúchas, The Heritage Service

ISBN 1 901233 68 5 (paper)
ISBN 1 901233 69 3 (bound)

Acknowledgements: to the following periodicals, where some of these poems, or versions of them, have been published: *Amethyst* (Canada); *Apertura* (Luxembourg); *Asylum; Céide; Chapman* (Scotland); *Cyphers; Fife Lines* (England); *Edinburgh Review* (Scotland); *Janus* (USA); *Kotaz* (South Africa); *Northeast Corridor* (USA); *New Orphic Review* (Canada); *Poetry Ireland Review; Podium; Pulsar* (England); *The Coffee House* (England); *The Holly Bough 2000; The Malahat Review* (Canada); *The Shop; The Southern Review* (USA); *The Steeple*. 'Gold Under Furze' was published in *Or Volge L'Anno: At The Years Turning*, ed, Marco Sonzogni (Dedalus, 1998). 'Brandon Is Clear', 'Metamorphosis' and 'A Dream Of Lapwings' were published in *Cúm: An Anthology of New Writing from Kerry*, ed. Moya Cannon (Kerry County Council, 1996). 'Good Friday Assemblage' was published in *Human Rights Have No Borders*, ed. Kenneth Morgan and Almut Schlepper (Marino Books, 1998, for Amnesty International).'Stroke' and 'Jasmine' were published in the author's collection, *Digging Towards The Light* (Dedalus, 1994).

Dedalus Press books are represented and distributed in the U.S.A. and Canada by **Dufour Editions Ltd.**, P.O. Box 7, Chester Springs, Pennsylvania 19425 and in the UK by **Central Books**, 99 Wallis Road, London E9 5LN

The Dedalus Press receives financial assistance from An Chomhairle Ealaíon, The Arts Council, Ireland.
Printed in Dublin by Colour Books Ltd

Contents

In memory of

Denis Bushe
(1918 - 1993)

WREN

The whirr of trapped panicky wings, a small
Thump, then silence. When I found you lying
In a double-glazed stupor near the window
And held you in my cupped hands, little king

Of all birds I thought you'd never live
Until Stephen's day to be caught in the furze.
To cover you and keep you warm was just
A kindness towards your quivering frailty.

So when, again unseen, you pushed aside
Your winding-sheet and whirred straight out
The open door, it was like found money
To hurry to the window and to see you,

Tail cocked, strutting your tiny stuff
In and out of crevices in a wall,
Exploring pockets of light and air
Between the weight and darkness of the stones.

And when you climbed the ladder of seed-pods
To sway and sing in the ruffling wind
My heart sang too, as if suddenly lifted
To majestic heights on an eagle's back.

January Epiphanies

Snow being rare here, I walked out early,
Hoping to concelebrate sunrise with music.
Rushes and furze stood stiff with amazement
And sallies experimented with the new weight

On their branches. Light tingled across fields
And crystals here and there sparkled an answer
Like an orchestra tuning up. As the sun cleared
The mountain behind me, it was almost dancing.

I had brought Sibelius for the Walkman,
So the sun became percussion and *Finlandia* boomed
Across the whole epic mile of snowy waste
Back to my house. I put the kettle on and hummed

The tune we sang in the pub last night, the one
Where the thrush and the robin their sweet notes entwine,
And when I pulled the curtains to check the bird-table,
My mind somewhere between Finland and Mooncoin,

A ruffle-feathered thrush was chasing a robin
Away from its share of the breadcrumbs and seeds.
They weren't entwining their sweet notes; but still,
Still, today is the Feast of the Epiphany.

A DRIVE TO EYRIES

For David Mason

I remember especially the acute
Blue light in which the islands floated,
Neither sea nor sky but an exhalation
Common to both yet full of astonishment.

That day, that journey, there was no horizon.
Sunlight bounced off the sea like words
And mountain roads wound around themselves
Like an endless conversation with God.

Time itself swung between the huge
Stone walls of the fort at Staigue,
Ponderous with age, and the bobbing
Plastic mussel-rafts at Kilmackilloge.

There was plenty of time, beyond Lauragh,
To digress and drive deep into a valley,
Delighted by the rhythm of the lake's
Iambic light and shadow through the trees.

Below the Healy Pass and Hungry Hill,
When I told you the valley's name,
You mean that it was here . . .? No, not *that* Glanmore,
Yet full of cadences, sonnets of brightness.

So here's to you, in midwinter Minnesota,
Cold, you tell me, inland and flat.
May you be flooded with light. Here
The December sea outside my window heaves

In grey and green under lowering clouds
And enclosing headlands, absorbing all
Shape, colour and the memory of sunlight.
Once again, there is no horizon.

Metamorphosis

I might have missed them, so still
The seals lay on the low-tide slabs.
But for the curve of a tail, the slow
Turn of a head, they were living rocks.

Splendidly pedestalled, they had no need
Of the huge theatricalities of light
Beamed from a hidden sun to play
Against massive atlantic clouds and sea.

So when my binoculars eclipsed
Cliffs, sky and all perspective,
I was absorbed into their salty rankness,
The folds and wrinkles of their grainy hides.

For hours they basked, while I workd
Doggedly in the garden. Afterwards,
The last sod turned, I watched the tide
In a rising swell break over them.

And seeing their hides grow silky with wetness,
I could feel a quickening into fluency
As they slid their heaviness off the rocks,
Undulating themselves easily into waves.

Footsteps On Croagh Patrick

The sun his eye-piece, God was a jeweller
Examining the islands spread on Clew Bay,
As we zigzagged up the pilgrims' path,

Easily at first, then breathlessly cursing
The sliding stones, eroded by frost
And the bare feet of pilgrimage.

Nearer the summit, the frozen snow
At last gave a grip to floundering boots
As we stumbled up through wind-packed drifts.

In the clean air, following the tracks
Of an earlier sightseer or pilgrim,
We circled the small, hunched chapel,

Its grey walls stippled with driven snow,
And marvelled at the compacted crystals,
Knee-deep in those footprints, reflecting

The Easter sky. And how they plod
Still through my mind, those high, blue
Footprints into the miraculous!

October Sunlight

Just this morning a heavy dew,
Maybe a first, tentative frost,
Dragged the sun out early
To play on the delighted grass.

Waterweight of sunlight
Hung in beads, in chimes,
Along each curving blade
Like something about to happen

Or that already has. Either way,
Rites of passage are in the air,
Which all at once is full
Of promise and of memory.

In my neighbour's meadow
New grass is shooting through
The ruts that tractors gouged
Making the late-cut silage.

And here at my house,
Among the withering stalks,
There's one garden daisy
Wide-eyed with reprieve.

PLANTING GARLIC

(i)

The tenth of January. I must be mad,
My neighbour says, as I prepare the ground.
But the gleam on pike after sunlit

Pikeful of seaweed belies the season,
Foresees the spring in the sodden earth
That clings in black lumps to my boots.

I mark my ridge, the spade awkward
In the sticky clay, then shovel up
From the furrow. The dark rectangle

Shapes itself slowly over the seaweed.
Now it will be drying, silently coaxing
The rich fronds towards their sweet decay.

(ii)

I prise open a bulb, my fingers
All at once releasing hints of sap
Like a memory in the frosty air.

The separated cloves look fit to burst
With newness, gleaming on the clay
Like stars that have dropped to earth.

Here, spread out, are feasts to come,
With mussels opening in anticipation,
Tomatoes and herbs racing to the smell!

And there will be the conjuring of summer
When the door of the shed creaks open
On plaited sunshine stored in airy bunches.

(iii)

And may there be no need for any cures,
No catch in the breath to be eased by infusions
Or a clove in red flannel around the neck,

Nor for a clove to be anxiously pressed
Into the shoes of children, to ward off
The hectic red cheeks of consumption,

Nor yet for the clove stitched tight
Into the tails of cattle, to purify
Blood and water against the black disease.

Now is my time for a cleansing of the blood.
Here, in this garden, this day and all
This magic is a cure beyond belief.

(iv)

Two inches deep, six inches apart,
The cloves pattern the soil. I repeat
The instructions like a mantra as I plant.

I sniff at the pungency that's charm
Against werewolves and vampires,
And I place my cloves in exorcism

Of all the darknesses I fear within
And without myself, and of all seasons
That would suck the light from the world.

And so to mark the limits of my patch
I drive a stake down into the ridge
And straight through the heart of winter.

STROKE

(i)

Stroke. The verb is gentle, whispering
Good news or bad with balanced intent,
The inevitable synonymous with the possible.

The noun's abruptness, on the other hand,
Announces arbitrary decrees, sudden strokes
Of pens, or whips, indifferently dispensed.

They both combined to form your sentence.
How gently you placed your feet when, delicate
As a bird, you dizzily walked the garden!

Even in the ambulance, the hospital,
The inch-by-inchness of your stroke at first
Deceived us, softened us into a routine

Of gathering for crumbs of reassurance.
For days, for weeks, we scattered or settled,
Brooding over our different hopes

Until the shell of potential cracked
Open, the verb turned to its noun
And stroke became its brutal fact.

(ii)

And how is he now? People would ask.
Day by day it grew more difficult
To answer. The questions seemed to be

Not really about you. Those puppet steps
You took, supported between physios,
Did they measure progress, or calibrate despair?

I remembered the long strides by hedges
When you stepped acres all over,
It seemed, every county in Ireland,

Valuing the land you had mapped out,
Every town, village and mileage spinning
Easily off your tongue. Now we watched you

Struggle to name familiar landmarks
We had passed on our way to visit.
There was no response I could carry home

To phone calls or neighbours who posed
The same unanswerable question: so how
Is he now? Much the same, I supposed.

(iii)

How endless are the vistas of hospitals!
Nurses disappearing down corridors, their laughter
Tinkling into silence. Wheelchairs silently

Moving along identical white passages.
Lifts humming non-stop between floors.
Even lying in your ward demanded

New perspectives. There was your bed and
The next one and the next one while you lay
And tried to understand your tubed and taped

Indignities. How could your battered brain not reel
Before such immensities! Climbers and divers
Who lose their lines and whose elements

Betray them into passages they had not mapped,
In panic or euphoria will grasp and plunge
Towards certainties they've left behind.

And so it was you turned your face
To walls that weren't there, and finding
No familiar limits, fell through space.

(iv)

Why am I in this peculiar position?
You asked in the physiotherapy gym
When you began a more circumspect

Conversation with your surroundings.
As the daily rotation lost its meaning
Your language grew in obliqueness.

Sometimes it was truer than the words
We hid behind: when I returned
Unexpectedly, to find you crying silently

And asked if it would help to talk,
You shook your head, waved me away.
I'm just bleeding, you said, from my eyes.

And when you raved about fire and danger,
Rambled about guards and prisoners of war,
You spoke the truth much plainer than we dared.

Realities which had escaped were caught,
Transformed. The world for you was image now,
And metaphor the final end of thought.

Jasmine

What colour is jasmine? you asked
Out of the blue from your wheelchair.
And suddenly the ward was filled
With the scent of possibility, hints
Of journeys to strange parts.

The question floored us. But the gulf
Was not the colours that we couldn't name
But that we couldn't recognise the road
Your question had travelled, nor sound the extent
Of the void to which it would return.

The ward remade itself in a hum
Of conscientious care. Outside, the usual
Traffic jams. We took the long way home.
Father, jasmine is a climbing plant
Whose flowers are normally white or yellow.

And may the fragrance of its blossoms twine
Around the broken trellises of your mind.

Brandon Is Clear!

It was all the forecast you ever needed:
Brandon is clear! you'd announce,
Get food for the journey. Sixpences in hand,
We ran for bulls' eyes, clove rocks, whatever
Would last us through those long drives
West of Dingle or around the Ring.

I've climbed Brandon since, known its dark cliffs
And cúms, the ambiguities of its mists,
But never before saw it so close, so clear
As it appeared the other day, around
A curve of the road, across the water,
Impossibly blue against a cloudless sky.

I hugged the wheel, still desperately praying
You'd had clear skies, sweets for your journey.

The Final Note

with gratitude to the staff of Our Lady's Hospice

It was, as they had promised, peaceful,
The other patients' beds quietly moved
Elsewhere for the time being, creating
More space, a sense of light.

Only once a fit of coughing wrenched
Open the coma, and your poor frightened eyes
Stared at or from some emptiness
Quickly spanned by a blessed needle.

And they moved and spoke softly in white,
Their practised love and consolation guiding
All our faltering steps to the shore,
A woman singing softly in your ear.

In the end, your breathing diminished
Like a note held vibrating to the point
Where the music heard is the music remembered
In a huge, expectant silence.

Funeral Mass

for Father John Kelly

You'd hardly have known yourself.
Never being one for the limelight,
You'd have sneaked away to the side,
Awkward but half-delighted, listening

To the discovery of consonances never before
So coherently noted. You'd have loved
The prayers and gifts of grandchildren,
The stories, birds, trees, sweets, games

And words naming and remembering
That best portion of a good man's life,
His little, nameless, unremembered acts
Of kindness and of love. And you always loved

The music played by a girl on a whistle,
Finding a rhythm for our processional steps,
Aching to sprinkle a blessing of order
On the rough inchoateness of our grief.

Pretence

In the middle of a rambling conversation,
I'm going, you sobbed, almost a wail.
I flinched, frightened of insight.

And where are you off to now? As if
My flippancy would divert you.
Across the water. The ward rocked.

I might have helped you steady your boat,
Talked about tides and currents, taken bearings,
Then pushed you out gently and waved.

But I floundered to the safety of pretence.
You that's terrified of aeroplanes
And even of ships, where would you be going?

You shifted in your wheelchair, wandering again.
I dragged my feet back through the shallows.

Alpine Path

Even if you had been here, you wouldn't
Ever have climbed the zigzag path
That rose sharply through the woods
With a steepness that was new to me.

You'd have been happier to stay below,
To wander through pastures exotic with cattle-bells
And cuckoo-song, and when you raised your eyes,
An occasional glimpse of faraway snow.

I thought of you as I struggled up,
Lungs and muscles increasingly aware
Of every step, yet still exulting
In the whole, breathless being there.

And I thought of how you would have loved
Especially the way the light slivered
Through the trees, and most especially
How it was caught and held intensely

In the green silk of the beeches
That canopied the path until, above the tree-line,
The same light spread, huge and unmediated,
On the scoured bareness of the high peaks.

From A Train

(i)

It was a bit the worse for wear, the train
That pulled itself laboriously out of Heuston
Towards the west. I tried to read.
Through drifts of fog we trundled slowly

Across the points at Portarlington.
For no reason but that sway and clatter
I remembered how much you loved the train,
The permutations of fields, even in winter.

Suddenly, I could almost hear you
Admonish me to put away my book
And look at what was passing by, the bogs,
The flooded meadows, the silhouetted trees.

(ii)

It always seemed a kind of magic when
You recognised the winter shapes of trees.
I never thought to match those skeletons
With the shape and shine of leaves and nuts

You would spill into my hands, my eyes
Absorbing what I missed of your half-heard
Words of explanation in the Phoenix Park
Or the Sunday afternoon by-roads of Meath.

The winged seeds that helicoptered
Exuberantly away from a sycamore,
The chestnut's candles and fishbone leaves,
Burnished conkers bursting from their shells,

Had no need of any larger pattern.
The shiny cups and grainy saucers
Of acorns clustered among serrated leaves,
Were complete in their own repetition.

(iii)

So much later, with you gone, so much
Was suddenly, lurchingly recognisable
When, as the jolting train left miles of track
Behind it across the sodden midlands,

Those bare outlines, unmistakably beech,
Clarified themselves out of the fog,
Lining an avenue that disappeared
Towards some stately home or another.

And as their newly familiar shapes
Receded into the distance, I recalled
How two parallel lines can never meet,
Except, perhaps, in their infinity.

Birdman

I remember your face, blank as an owl's,
In all that aimless busyness of therapy,
And my frustration, moving towards despair,
As the physio prompted your right hand
To your left shoulder, or the blue star
Into the yellow box, and you fumbled
And tried to wave the whole thing away.

And I remember how your head suddenly cocked
When, on a hunch, I showed you the bird-chart,
And how, at my tentative *Show me a blackbird,*
Now show me a swallow, your finger rose and circled
And stabbed time after time, as casually accurate
As a sparrow picking at seed, a heron spearing fish,
Or a crow tearing a rabbit crushed by passing wheels.

Christmas Shopping List

For my wife I order that the sun
Be freshly squeezed each morning of her life,
That the moon attend ceremoniously
On all of her comings and goings
And that the stars should never cease
Doing the rounds of her eyes.

For my daughter I command that roads
Be laid smoothly between mountains,
That rivers echo guidance along valleys,
That a fair wind rise to bring her
In good time again and again to swim
In the morning waves of her childhood.

For my son let the satellites beam
Messages of love precisely here and there
For the time being, and the grids that net
The seas and continents direct him
To all the co-ordinates he chooses,
Then catch and trawl him home.

And for myself if all of this
Might come to pass in seven days
What more could I want? I would know
That I was right to have ideas
Above my station, and I would
Be complete and know that it was good.

19 December 1999

Postcard From Hospital

Just a few post-observation lines to say
Your diagnosis was spot-on. All samples,
Syringes, charts and consultants now confirm
The diabetes you nagged so patiently about.

So this is just to thank you and your blood's
Worth bottling too. Forgive the sour words.
All I could hear was a threatening buzz
And, shying from imagined stings,

I slapped uselessly at myself, forgot
The rich slow dripping in the comb.
Now I must find a new path to the hive
And savour every taste along the way.

I'll be home soon, complete with my prognosis,
Craving mouth upon mouthful of your sweetness.

A Dream of Lapwings

All day, as we walked the island,
Lapwings cavorted in the wind, or carried
Their crested silhouettes from rock to rock,
Mewing between heather and sheep-cropped grass.

You once dreamed, you said, of a great lapwing
That with huge wingbeats and rippling plumage
Carried you high over familiar mountains
While you clung to the iridescence of its crest.

Later, as we lay drowsy after love
High among the cliff-top buttercups,
Lapwings in high-pitched abandon above us
Played your dream again. I could see

The hugencss of your flight above a valley,
How it brought people streaming out of doors
To marvel at the shadow, and to feel
The beneficence of those passing wings.

Holiday Poem

The cheek of you, leaning out
To open shutters and pour sunlight

Over last night's wine and clothes.
The marsh where yesterday

We gathered sea-lavender and caught
The kingfisher's rainbow darts

Stretches in birdcalls below you
Leaning out, bare-arsed over Brittany.

An Alpine Flora

When, at last, breathless,
We reached that high plateau of love,

The blue gentians opened
Wider and deeper with wonder,

While the little nameless pink ones
Blushed with delight in the limestone fissures,

And the wild strawberries blossomed,
Heady with the promise of fruit.

There's Gold Under Furze

Bíonn ór faoin aiteann, the saying goes;
And went, like all the sayings from this townland
To take their rest, indexed and catalogued,
In the archives of a folklore department.

The scattered clumps of furze, that had staked out
Evidence of fertile ground, are spendthrift now,
Throwing fool's gold over impoverished fields
That once had notions of prosperity.

As with the sayings, so with the voices,
Those who were chatterers and those who chewed
Words with relish, or spat them out
In gossip, politics or tried and tested feuds.

They had stories too, that sometimes tumbled over
Into song, of seals in caves, miraculous
Streams of milk, and how their own Liberator
Fooled all the clever Englishmen in London

They recalled the fishermen who stayed out all night,
Rising and falling on a fog-bound swell,
Because the lights that beckoned them ashore
Were waving from a world that wished them harm.

Such voices shortened winter. Now these fields,
Their network of gapped and crumbling stone walls
Like the braincells of a disintegrating mind,
Have forgotten the voices that gave them names.

At least there's no winter here. Winter
Has migrated to the city. In the summer,
Holiday homes in tasteful stone share solitude
With larks, the golden furze, and other silences.

Good Friday Assemblage

Here is a new sculpture, not magnificently
Bronze, nor pedestalled on granite.
This is tinkering, gathering, an assemblage.

Here is a bolt coaxed where it doesn't belong,
With exquisite care not to shear the thread.
Here are dirty hands, and coarse cleansing.

This is a sculpture of midnight phone calls,
Of walk-outs and re-draftings and strategies.
Here is the ache of many twisted arms.

This is a sculpture that has been spun
And doctored and bandaged and splinted.
Here are crutches, oil for hurt egos, cures.

Here are the disposable pens of civil servants
Who rewrite tablets we thought were made of stone.
Here are computers that move words like mountains

Here are paramilitaries fine-tooth-combing paragraphs,
Teasing out the nuances and defining the parameters
That will allow their heads to stay above the parapet.

Here are the strands too complicated to follow,
And here are the weavers, honoured at last:
Here are the politicians, really making shapes.

And the sculptors walk, amazed, around their work,
Not sure of what to say, realising there's no need
For the statues they love to be cast in a furnace.

11 April, 1998

MILITARY ROAD

Aerial photography from a strutted bi-plane
No doubt made the outline of its route
Perfectly clear at the time. Even now

This military road is by a long way
The easiest track through these mountains,
Much safer than the steep, narrow paths.

Buttressed with stone and wide enough
For horse-drawn carts and artillery,
It winds around the cliffs and gorges

And snakes its way right over the top
To the high plateau where, among the pines,
It arrives at a squat, crumbling fort.

From there, steeper paths will bring you down
Quickly to the villages, and rows of crosses
With small brass plates, in many languages.

Headland Storm

Shouldering the doors of the car open
Into the thump and drag of the gale,
Our faces whipped by frenzied hood-strings,

We push our way to a wall, the remains
Of a turf-stack a dusty madness,
And stare at a sea that's out of its mind.

Below us, the huge waves thud
Sickeningly into caves, where once
A strain of seals wailing twined itself

Into tunes that seemed taken off the wind,
Songs that ached for changelings to return
To the hearth, its familiar stories.

Empty houses shrink into themselves.
The storm flings spray like stones
At unresponding windows, dripping windows.

Now angling ourselves against the gale,
Now frog-marched helpless in its grip,
We zigzag up the steep bóithrín

To where, suddenly, we can breathe.
The tops of bushes convulse themselves
Above the small bowl of calm

That holds a deserted farmhouse
Comfortably in against the hill,
Terra firma in a sea of wind.

They had an eye for shelter here,
Choosing the site in winter storms,
Positioning corner stones in summer.

But the diviners of shelter
And the adjudicators of winds
Are long gone from this hill.

The wind is tearing through
Its network of small stone walls,
And its fields have forgotten their names.

BEAR

Was it a curator's hype or a shaman's
Breath misting the glass cases
That gave the name *Art and Magic*
To this exhibition of Eskimo artefacts?

They are ordinary and exquisite
Enough for anything, these figurines
In whale-bone, tusk and driftwood,
Animals and birds of all types, and none.

The Tunit who carved them have vanished
Centuries ago into archaeology
And cannot adjudicate on the catalogue
That says *Bear: floating or flying figure.*

It's easy to see that stretched bone nose
Etching a huge V on a mirror of arctic sea.
But flying? And still, I share the curator's
Hankering after totems and the journeying of souls.

This is no matter. Art *is* the magic
Of craftsman and shaman, and this bear's
True element is the mind through which it moves,
As through a crystal of sea and ice and sky.

Didjeridoo

No doubt it was the baby, the business
Of sites, plans, house and all
The attendant satisfaction that pushed it

From our minds, beyond the 'final notice'.
I had never collected it from Customs, away back,
After we had flown home, the package labelled

'Aboriginal artefact' that had followed by sea.
Now and again I thought of it, wondering
If it lay choked with dust, silently shelved

With the other veterans of the yearly auction.
I hope it resounded for someone, or that children
Spied each other wide-eyed along its length.

Twenty years on, increasingly I imagine it,
The bark incised with criss-cross patterns,
Its snakes and emus sacred in ochre.

I would search with it for songlines, despite
The mockery of kookaburras, the rasp
Of cicadas, the sun beating like a drum.

I would hum new totems into my dreaming,
Feel the pulsing in the lizard's throat
And root for grubs between huge horizons.

I would leave my handprint at the mouths of caves
And I would feel, far beyond the last fence
The reverberation of the earth aching for rain.

Hawk

Over Annaghmakerrig a hawk's wings
Caught winter sunlight above the trees.
Between the woods the fields were blank
With snow. The hawk quartered the ground.

Back in my room the lamplit page
Spread white before me. Nothing stirred
In the silence between. I remembered
The hawk, its methodical hunger.

PEREGRINE

(i)

When it dropped
Out of nowhere
On the black and white
Dreamflight of oystercatchers

The belly-feathers scattered
Like a burst pillow,
Catching the light
As they settled on grass

And a dark wing twitched
Uselessly in protest,
Refusing to waken
To this sunlit nightmare.

(ii)

Click. I zoom inexpertly
As the head lifts
And turns towards me
From the casual
Disembowelment. Steady the lens. Click.

Unblinking. I supply the cliché
The shake in my lens won't capture.

Click. I supply also
The sharp focus turned
On me, divining a horror
Deep in my entrails.
Click. Again and again.

(iii)

Against the light, against the silvered waves,
The silhouetted victim hangs from the dark
Wings and straining talons that hooded crows
Shadow and harry with an eye for the main chance.

Here is the end of pride and plume. Flapping
At random towards arbitrary closings,
The raucous procession twists and turns
Against the silvered waves, against the light.

Ballyheigue Revisited

Heartyheads we called them, and you lay
Prone beside a rockpool to fish them,
Dangling a bent, barbless pin on a thread,
A piece of leathery *báirneach* for your bait.

First the transparent shrimp in sudden darts
Came gathering around the bait, their little
Tentative nosings vibrating up the thread.
Electric shockers, we said, in tingling delight.

But they were nothing to the heartyhead
That glided out from underneath a ledge,
Brushing aside seaweed and anemones,
Opening his fat mouth towards the bait.

And then you pulled and almost always
He slipped off the pin. But now and again
You tugged him free of the pool and you stood
And whirled him round, scattering water

In triumphant, sunlit wheels, racing
Impossible distances across the sky
Until you slowed gradually, and anxious
To begin again you knelt and let him go.

More than thirty years later, as I picked
My steps over the same textures of rock—
The ribbed ones that were hard to walk, the smooth
Purple ones that held the heat of the sun —

He took my breath away, that boy —
Intent over the pool, the same
Red curls I once longed to grow out of —
Who looked at me incuriously for a moment

While something barbed and unimaginable
Tugged, and I was rooted to the spot.

Guide Dog

For Mollie Coffey

I'm only scribbling in the shadows now,
You wrote, asking for a poem
About the Inny Strand, once better

Than a whole world of tranquillisers,
But beyond you now, you said,
Unless you get a guide dog.

So here's this guide dog, scratching
At the backdoor of your memory.
Just wrap yourself in something warm

And let yourself out. Whisper your own
Private commands and he'll bring you
Easily through the fields to the strand

Dreaming in spring moonlight, or washed
Clean and hard by winter tides.
On limpid June days you'll see

Men in seine-boats, shoulders tensed
For the salmon's splash that'll send
The oars straining to circle the shoal.

If it's warm and the tide is low
You can walk across the ferry,
Carrying your shoes in your hand.

While you sit down to watch the swell
Breaking over Carraig Éanna or The Blue Boys
And recall a verse of *Mo Shlán Beo Soir,*

Your dog will walk through pools of reflection,
Leaving long trails of pawmarks
Across huge skies and passing clouds.

He'll chase seagulls that have settled
Stiffly in rows along the tide-line
Like forgotten years, scattering them

Into urgencies of strident protest
At his delirious barking and abandoned
Spray-scattering race through the waves.

And when he brings you home again
And scratches at the door, let yourself
Back in and put the kettle on the range.

Bolus

i.m. Máire Uí Chinnseala

At Bolus, where on a pet day we parked,
At the end of the road, high over the sea,
You sat out in a folding chair, you the walker,

Who in your health had never bothered with drives
Or views, or nuisances like the binoculars
You now focused on distant islands. And then:

Well, this is just paradise! I flinched away,
Hearing your words beat their huge black wings
Against the fragile day. But when I turned

Your wasting face was radiantly matter-of-fact
And that cacophonous irony I'd heard
Was echoing only inside my humbled mind.

I remake that day now, and see it plain,
Rinsed clear of all ironies, see you
Fold up your chair and walk, into wholeness.

Isolated Being

after Louis le Brocquy

If there are praying hands, they are raised
Still dripping paint from the viscera,
And the ethereal brushstrokes of the head
Descend towards the deep shadow at the thighs.

If there is substance in the central warmth
And lumpiness of those yellows and reds,
It is realised in their constant absorption
Towards the high, translucent white on blue.

Isolated being, companion of my youth,
Veiled envoy between earth and stars,
Discovered again, you teach me still
That nothing is one without the other.

THE WIDOWED BRIDE'S LAMENT

A translation of Caoineadh Liam Uí Raghallaigh

Do you remember it still, that day
The village was alive with horsemen
And there were clergy of every rank
All gathering for my marriage?
The fiddle was played at table
While a harp was lightly fingered
And three white-robed women waited
To convey my love to our bed.

To be widowed while still a virgin —
This was the end of my youth.
Bring the story to my people
That my treasure of treasures is drowned.
Had I been in that boat, that day,
My two hands tight on the rope,
I swear on my married name
There'd be no cause for this grief.

It's no wonder that this story
Has your mother and father racked
And is a torture in the breast
Of the woman who nursed your childhood,
Let alone your wedded wife
Who never once arranged your bed,
Since your journey from the shore
Was to be a journey without return.

Sea-worms crawl through your empty eyes
And your lips are eaten by crabs
While the foraging shoals of salmon
Push your soft white hands aside.
I'd give anything to escape
From the repetition of this vision
And the pathetic life that is mine now,
Single in everything but my name!

FINAL VERSION

i.m. Michael Hartnett

Too early. Yes, all of that. But now you've said
A farewell to all language, and are translated
To a version where, definitively yourself,
Sharing elements with hares and otters,
And raising pewter mugs with spailpín poets,
You can hear the pulse-music you knew well
Lies beyond all poems, and before them,
And cannot be lost in translation.

Hopkins on Skellig Michael

(i) Landing

By Christ then but Skellig will test that poor man!
The boatmen dug their oars deep in the swell
And pulled the bow around. *Upon my soul*
He'll know his prayers well after a night
Up there on the cliffs with the screeching birds.
It's a different man we'll be collecting then!
They waved towards the diminishing black figure
Who had knelt to pray on the small pier.
Just like a stranded cormorant, they chuckled,
And bent their backs to the oars.
                                        On the pier,
Father Gerard Hopkins had begun his retreat
At the very edge of Europe. *But from what*
Am I retreating? Why do I compound
My exile here in the most extreme corner
Of this most extreme land? England, Ireland,
Have disappeared with that boat and I am here.
He remembered the boatmen telling a boy
To carry *the minister's bags*, their disbelief
That his collar was Catholic, the muttered aside
About *a fierce Protestant accent for a priest.*

Head bowed, he endured again the everyday
Claws of exile, the scratches of no harm meant.

(ii) Steps

Steps.
Stone steps.
Steps
Cut into stone.
Step
After stone step.
Steps
Of stone slabs.
Slab
After worn stone slab.
Edge of stone.
Step
The edges of stone.
Step
The edges of soul.
My soul
Is stone, is splintered slate.
O let my slow
Plodding
Hone me,
Edge me with brightness.

(iii) Saddle

Christ's Saddle, he remembered, is the dip
Between the islands' two peaks, just before
The final ascent. *You can rest there, Father,*
And gather yourself to go to the top.
Breath seared and legs ached as he sank
Into the sea-campion. Rabbits scattered
Into myriad burrows at the intrusion
And gulls sheered away in raucous protest.
The wind and the querulous birds seemed
To play one and the same note of mockery.
Christ's Saddle. He started at the sudden
Reverberation of the name among the rocks,
Remembering how once in Wales a bird
Had ridden the wind like Christ in glory
While fire broke, lovely and dangerous.
He closed his senses, became a darkness
That curled interminably around itself,
Squeezed brain, body and soul to all or nothing,
Then howled its wounded self deep into the wind.

(iv) Final Flight

The whole island rose to form a buttress
For the last, exposed steps to the monastery.
Flight, he thought, was the wrong word,
Too easy for these hard-hewn stairs that seemed
To lead to nowhere but their own sheer
Infinity, winding through vertical
Planes where the eye was constantly drawn up
Or dizzily down. The horizons of everyday
Vanished between firmament and abyss.
His mind lurched too, hung once again
Above unfathomed falls, sheer and frightful.

Endure, he whispered, *I will yet endure,*
And crept on hands and knees towards the comfort
Of the high stone cells, out of the wind.

(v) Enclosure

And then to follow the path, level at last,
Across a narrow ledge and to enter
Under huge lintels, the enclosure! A small
Miracle of terracing, and the stone cells
Shaped like beehives, like bells, and all
The air was honey, was chimes, was harmony.
To fall on his knees by the high cross
Where the east to west pitch of the oratory
Encompassed the whole world, while gannets
Circled widely above silvering seas
And all the spheres meshed, was to rise
With the grace of a bird and to wheel
In the infinite circles of God's mind.

(vi) Source

They're never dry, those miraculous wells
Right in the heart of the monastery,
He had been told. And there they were,
Full of brackish water. He willed belief,
But curiosity welled stronger in him,
Who had probed the inscape of bluebells,
Patterned a lunar halo, and diaried
How canal water squeezed itself through a lock.
Investigation quickly undermined the miraculous,
Undammed the secrets of the underground
Conduits from the slabs behind the cells,
Grooved and guided into the stone basins.
A miracle still, he mused, of intent,
Of will to stay, of work, to channel
Water through stone as grace through spirit.
Laborare orare est. Aqua vita est.

(vii) Storm

Squall after squall from the black north-west,
Layer upon layer of darkness, stratum
Down stratum of stone-faced time, all
Without rhyme or reason pounded him,
Beat him level in the blurred vastness
Of the storm. The monastery terrace
Was tilting like a panicking deck,
The island was riven stone, splintering
On the shipwreck of itself, itself
Its own cause and cacophonous effect,
Foundering deeper into its own void.
Rain-and-spray blinded, he stumbled to the high
Cross, clung to it, swallowed salt,
Conjured witness, summoned arbitration
Against blankness.
                                        The lighthouse beam flickered
Behind walls of rain, beat against clouds.
Light beat then, too, in his brain, spread
The length of passages smeared with despair,
And sprang in salty relief to his eyes.

Enough, he prayed. *Let me elect to follow*
And light, though it comes and goes, will shine.
Will the clarion, and the clarion will sound.

And this bare brute, air-bruised, wind-weary and wounded,
Floundered towards light once whole, whole once again.

(viii) Etymology

Praying, trying to transform morning
Into matins, he was shaken by the screech
Of a peregrine falcon, as a burst puffin
Scattered over the path his office took.
He laid aside the missal, looked for paradigms.

He could see a derivation in the abrupt
Latin, *falx: sickle*, realising those talons
That sliced down layers of brightness
In that appalling plunge, those bloody feathers.
But what consoling pattern could he find
In the *haecceitas* of curved beak tearing flesh
Here, now, on this fanged Atlantic rock?

None, none, in the sickle alone,
Shining or bloodstained, meaningless,
A surd.

Search then, for meaning among other elements.

Peregrine. Wanderer. Per agria.
Wanderer across lands. Peregrinus.
In Roman law, stateless. A stranger.

Wingbeats about his head, clawings at his brain.

Peregrinus. Peregrinatio. Pro Christo.
Peregrinatio pro Christo. Exile .
Pilgrim. Pilgrimage for Christ. For Christ
A stranger, removed, becomes pilgrim,

Becomes hawk, like Christ, like Christ, a victim,
Is hawk and victim and in Christ's sacrifice
Is one with the world won all at once back.

And he prayed that his ultimate fall might be cushioned
By the hawk sacrificed, in the plumage of Christ.

(ix) Empires

Among the stone cells, he considered Empire,
Its porticoes and columns, its bronze statues
In sunlit squares dispensing jurisprudence
Flanked by cannon, the dust of savagery
Settling under the weight of Latin words,
And found it good. He yearned for Latin prayers
To be its yeast, to quicken power into praise
Of the One, Holy Catholic and Apostolic.
He craved the centres, mourned for himself,
Stranded, swept from their chronicles and courts
Among people who broke bread with him only
By divine accident, a confusion of history.

The noon sun burnt mist away, settled wind,
Drew heat from bare stone. He found a niche,
And, almost comfortable, eased himself into it.
The sun and the night's exhaustion closed his eyes.
Margins and centres merged, half-dreamt, on the peak.
Rome and London spun a globe between them.
Imperium! Imperium! boomed the sun,
As its light dissolved, shimmering, in the waves.

(x) Leaving

By God, he doesn't look too bad. Bobbing
In the shadow of the rock they hauled
Fish after shining fish aboard. They watched
As he descended slowly from the summit
And heard him call out something to them.
He can wait awhile now. There's a shoal here!
They laughed, spilling out more mackerel.
At last, tired, they pulled ashore, half-expecting
Recriminations, protests of neglect.
But at the pier he waved, and smiled
As they spun the boat showily alongside.
He settled easily on a scaly thwart
And eyed the quivering, thumping fish.
An appropriately miraculous catch, gentlemen,
He offered buoyantly. They smiled politely,
Sensing a joke they did not understand.

There wasn't much talk as they rowed home.
They established he hadn't been too lonely
Or frightened, and all agreed they were blessed
With the calm day after such a bad night.